Impressum
Verlag: BABADADA GmbH, Nedderfeld 112 , 22529 Hamburg
Geschäftsführer / Verlagsleitung: Harald Hof
Druck: Books on Demand GmbH, In de Tarpen 42, 22848 Norderstedt

Imprint
Publisher: BABADADA GmbH, Nedderfeld 112 , 22529 Hamburg, Germany
Managing Director / Publishing direction: Harald Hof
Print: Books on Demand GmbH, In de Tarpen 42, 22848 Norderstedt

學校

school

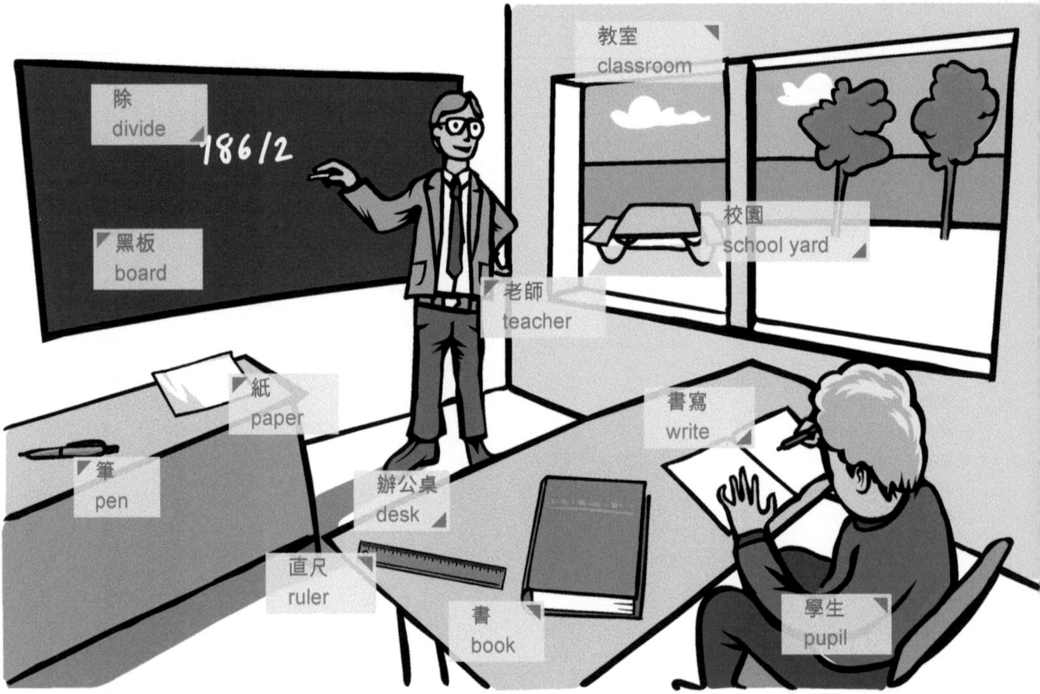

教室
classroom
除
divide
186/2
黑板
board
校園
school yard
老師
teacher
紙
paper
書寫
write
筆
pen
辦公桌
desk
直尺
ruler
書
book
學生
pupil

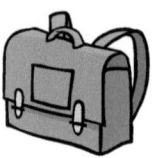

書包

satchel

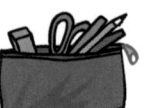

鉛筆盒

pencil case

鉛筆

pencil

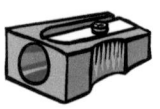

削鉛筆機

pencil sharpener

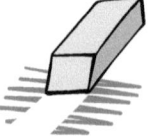

橡皮擦

rubber

畫板

drawing pad

圖畫
drawing

畫筆
paintbrush

顏料盒
paint box

剪刀
scissors

膠水
glue

練習冊
exercise book

家庭作業
homework

12

數字
number

2+2

加
add

5-2

減
subtract

2×2

乘
multiply

計算
calculate

A

字母
letter

ABCDEFG
HIJKLMN
OPQRSTU
VWXYZ

字母表
alphabet

hello

字
word

課文
text

讀
read

粉筆
chalk

上課
lesson

登記
register

考試
exam

證書
certificate

校服
school uniform

教育
education

百科全書
encyclopedia

大學
university

顯微鏡
microscope

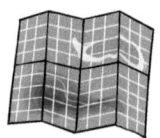

地圖
map

廢紙簍
waste-paper basket

旅行

travel

飯店
hotel
Grand
青年旅社
hostel
ROOMS
外幣兌換處
bureau de change
CHANGE
手提箱
suitcase
汽車
car

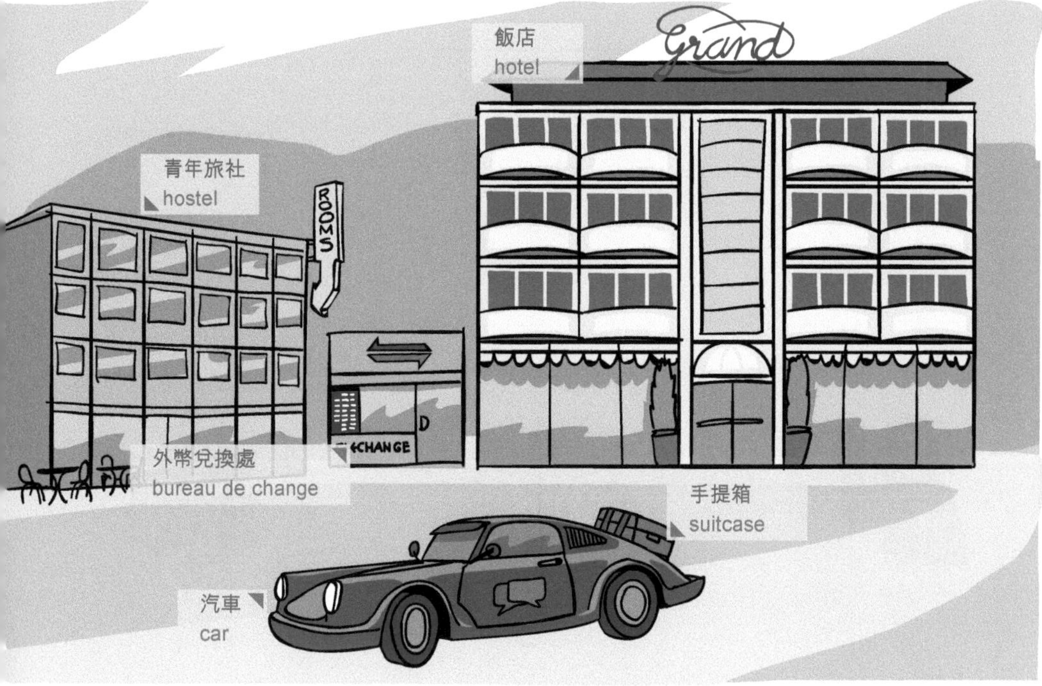

語言

language

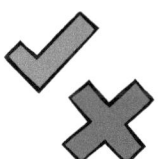

是/否

yes / no

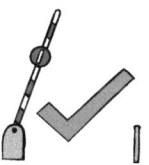

好的

Okay

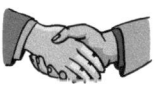

您好

hello

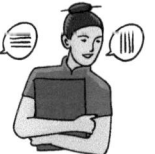

翻譯人員

translator

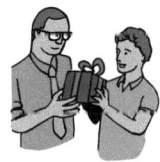

謝謝

Thank you

......多少錢？

how much is...?

我不明白

I do not understand

問題

problem

晚上好！

Good evening!

早上好！

Good morning!

晚安！

Good night!

再見

bye bye

方向

direction

行李

luggage

包

bag

背包

backpack

客人

guest

房間

room

睡袋

sleeping bag

帳篷

tent

旅行資訊

tourist information

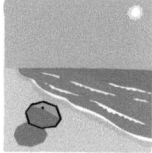

海灘

beach

信用卡

credit card

早餐

breakfast

午餐

lunch

晚餐

dinner

票

ticket

電梯

lift

郵票

stamp

邊界

border

海關

customs

大使館

embassy

簽證

visa

護照

passport

交通運送

transport

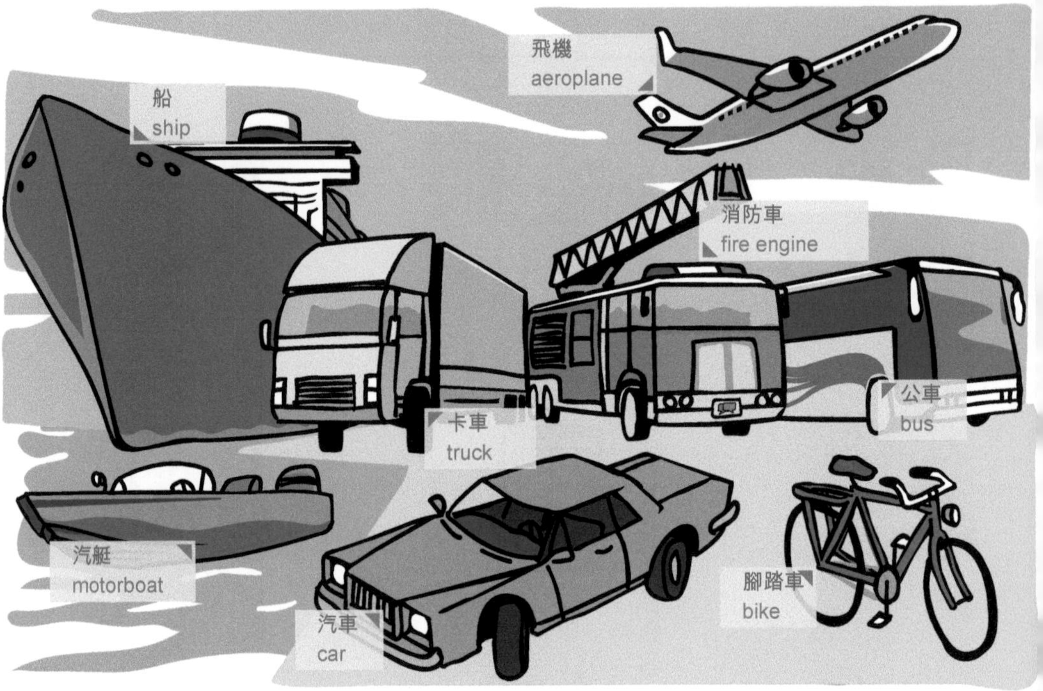

飛機
aeroplane
船
ship
消防車
fire engine
公車
bus
卡車
truck
汽艇
motorboat
腳踏車
bike
汽車
car

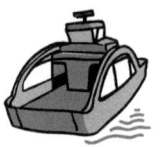

渡輪

ferry

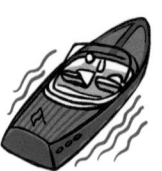

小船

boat

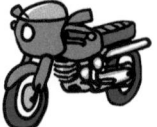

機車

motorbike

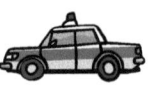

警車

police car

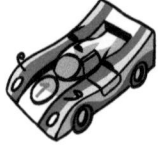

賽車

racing car

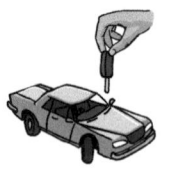

租車

rental car

拼車

car sharing

拖車

breakdown truck

垃圾車

refuse truck

馬達

motor

汽油

fuel

加油站

petrol station

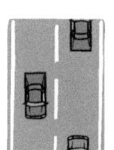

交通標識

traffic sign

交通

traffic

交通堵塞

traffic jam

停車場

car park

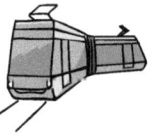

火車站

train station

軌道

tracks

火車

train

路面電車

tram

客車廂

carriage

直升機
helicopter

機場
airport

塔
tower

乘客
passenger

集裝箱
container

紙板箱
carton

手推車
cart

籃子
basket

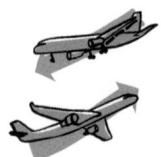

起飛/降落
take off / land

城市
city

村莊
village

市中心
city centre

房子
house

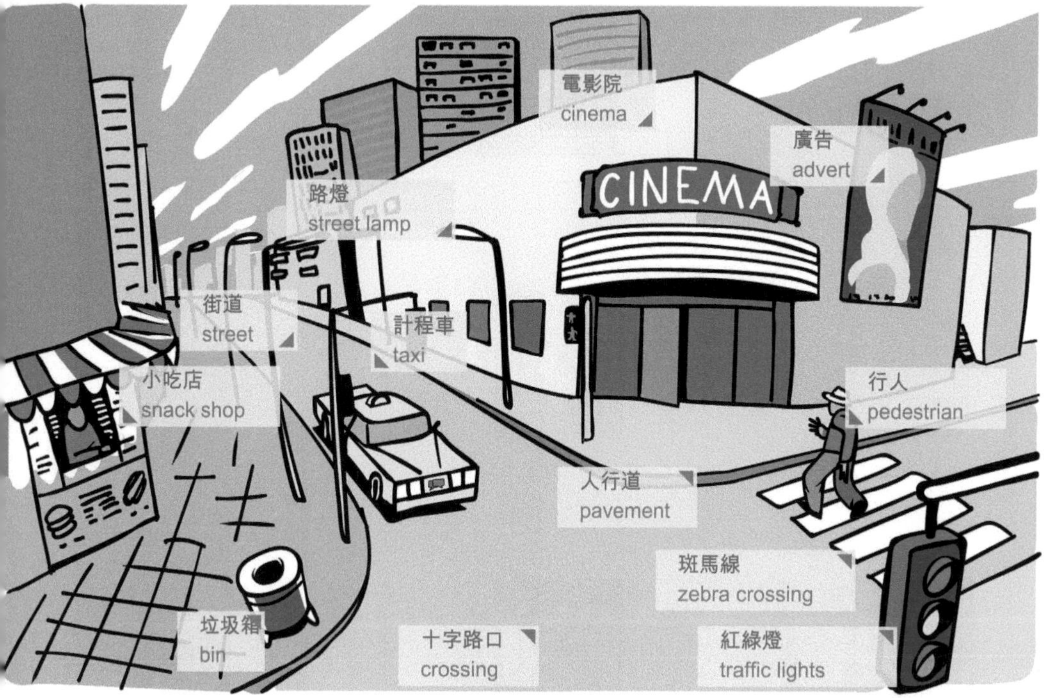
CINEMA
電影院
cinema
廣告
advert
路燈
street lamp
街道
street
計程車
taxi
小吃店
snack shop
行人
pedestrian
人行道
pavement
斑馬線
zebra crossing
垃圾箱
bin
十字路口
crossing
紅綠燈
traffic lights

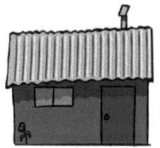

小屋

hut

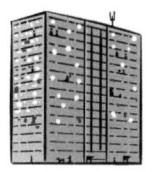

公寓

flat

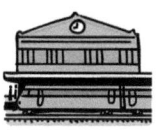

火車站

train station

市政廳

town hall

MUSEUM

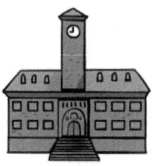

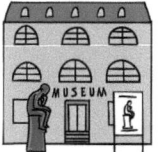

博物館

museum

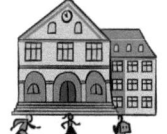

學校

school

大學

university

銀行

bank

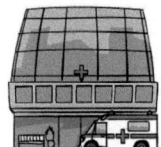

醫院

hospital

飯店

hotel

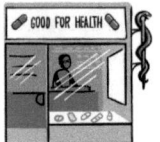

藥房

pharmacy

辦公室

office

書店

book shop

商店

shop

花店

florist's

超市

supermarket

市場

market

百貨商店

department store

魚店

fishmonger's

購物中心

shopping centre

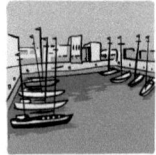

海港

harbour

公園

park

長凳

bench

橋

bridge

樓梯

stairs

捷運

underground

隧道

tunnel

公車站

bus stop

酒吧

bar

餐館

restaurant

郵筒

postbox

路標

street sign

停車計時器

parking meter

動物園

zoo

游泳池

swimming pool

清真寺

mosque

農場
farm

污染
pollution

墓地
graveyard

教堂
church

操場
playground

寺廟
temple

地形
landscape

樹葉
leaf

指示牌
signpost

路
way

草地
meadow

石頭
stone

樹
tree

徒步旅行
者
hiker

河
river

草
grass

花
flower

峽谷
valley

丘陵
hill

湖
lake

森林
forest

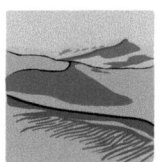

沙漠
desert

火山
volcano

城堡
castle

彩虹
rainbow

蘑菇
mushroom

棕櫚樹
palm tree

蚊子
mosquito

蒼蠅
fly

螞蟻
ant

蜜蜂
bee

蜘蛛
spider

地形 - landscape

甲蟲

beetle

青蛙

frog

松鼠

squirrel

刺蝟

hedgehog

野兔

hare

貓頭鷹

owl

鳥

bird

天鵝

swan

野豬

boar

鹿

deer

麋鹿

moose

水壩

dam

風力發電機

wind turbine

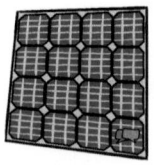

太陽能電池板

solar panel

氣候

climate

餐館
restaurant

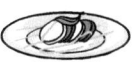

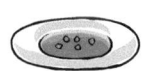

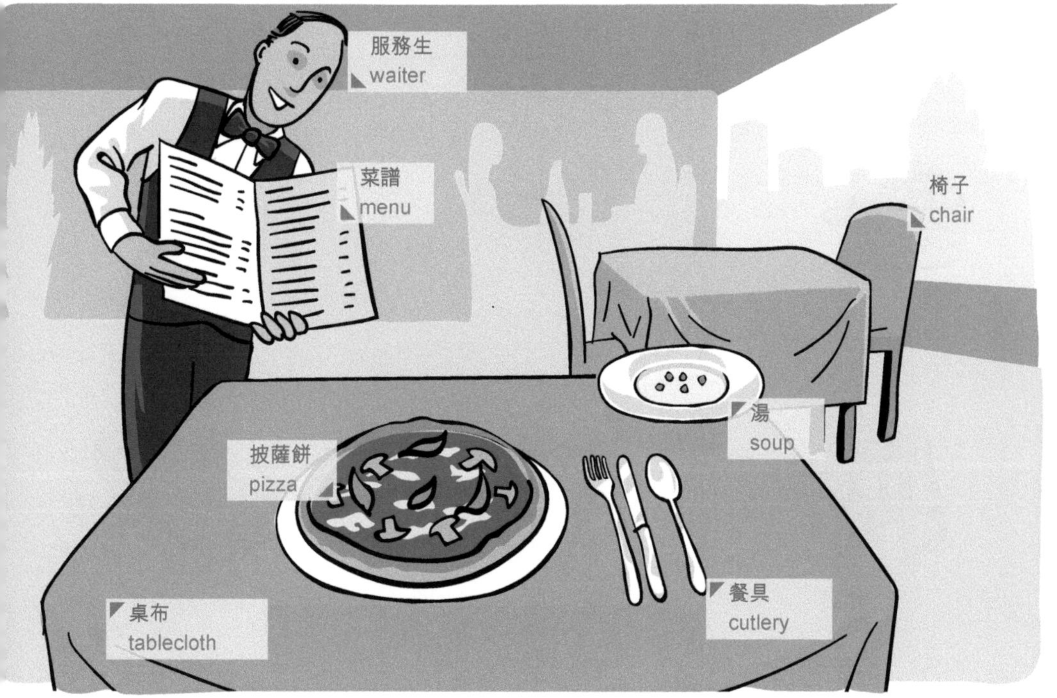
服務生
waiter
菜譜
menu
椅子
chair
湯
soup
披薩餅
pizza
桌布
tablecloth
餐具
cutlery

前菜

starter

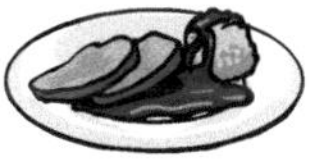

主菜

main course

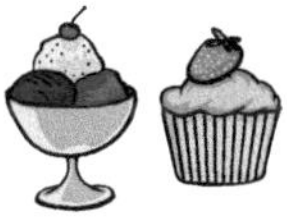

甜點

dessert

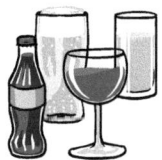

飲料

drinks

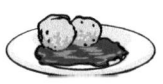

食物

food

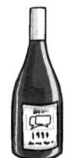

瓶子

bottle

速食

fast food

街邊小吃

street food

茶壺

teapot

糖盒

sugar bowl

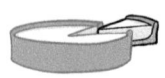

一份飯菜

portion

義式咖啡機

espresso machine

高腳椅

high chair

帳單

bill

托盤

tray

刀

knife

餐叉

fork

勺子

spoon

茶匙

teaspoon

餐巾

serviette

玻璃杯

glass

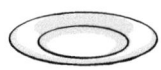

碟子
plate

湯盤
soup plate

碟子
saucer

醬
sauce

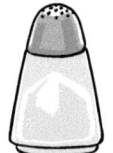

鹽瓶
salt pot

胡椒研磨罐
pepper mill

醋
vinegar

食用油
oil

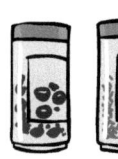

調味料
spices

番茄醬
ketchup

芥末
mustard

美乃滋
mayonnaise

超市

supermarket

特價
special offer
FOR
顧客
customer
乳製品
dairy
水果
fruit
購物車
trolley

BUTCHERS

肉鋪

butcher´s

BAKERY

麵包店

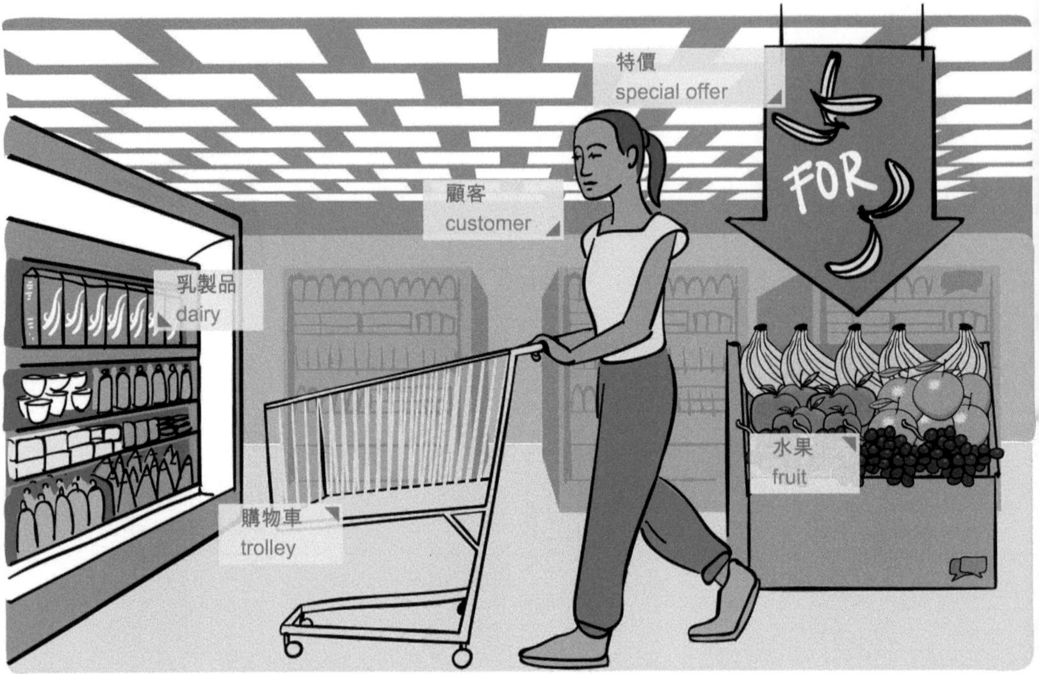

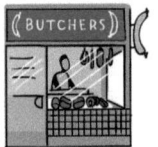

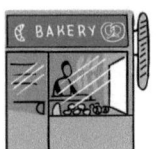

baker´s

稱重

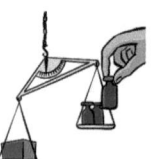

weigh

蔬菜

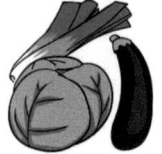

vegetables

肉

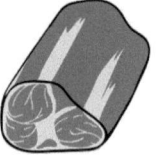

meat

冷凍食品

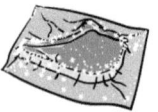

frozen food

冷盤
cold meat

罐頭食品
tinned food

洗衣粉
washing powder

甜食
sweets

日用品
household products

清潔用品
cleaning products

銷售員
salesperson

收銀機
till

收銀員
cashier

購物清單
shopping list

開放時間
opening hours

錢包
wallet

信用卡
credit card

袋子
bag

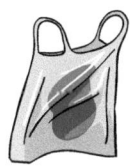

塑膠袋
plastic bag

水

water

果汁

juice

牛奶

milk

可樂

coke

紅酒

wine

啤酒

beer

酒

alcohol

可可

cocoa

茶

tea

咖啡

coffee

義式濃縮咖啡

espresso

卡布奇諾

cappuccino

香蕉

banana

蘋果

apple

柳丁

orange

西瓜

melon

檸檬

lemon

胡蘿蔔

carrot

大蒜

garlic

竹子

bamboo

洋蔥

onion

蘑菇

mushroom

堅果

nuts

麵條

noodles

義大利麵

spaghetti

米飯

rice

沙拉

salad

薯條

chips

炸馬鈴薯

fried potatoes

披薩餅

pizza

漢堡

hamburger

三明治

sandwich

炸豬排

cutlet

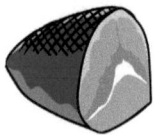

火腿

ham

義大利臘腸

salami

香腸

sausage

雞肉

chicken

烤肉

roast

魚

fish

燕麥片

porridge oats

木斯里

muesli

玉米片

cornflakes

麵粉

flour

牛角麵包

croissant

麵包捲

bread roll

麵包

bread

吐司

toast

餅乾

biscuits

奶油

butter

凝乳

curd

蛋糕

cake

蛋

egg

煎蛋

fried egg

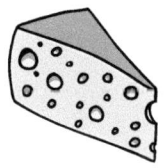

起司

cheese

冰淇淋

ice cream

糖

sugar

蜂蜜

honey

果醬

jam

巧克力醬

chocolate spread

咖哩

curry

農場
farm

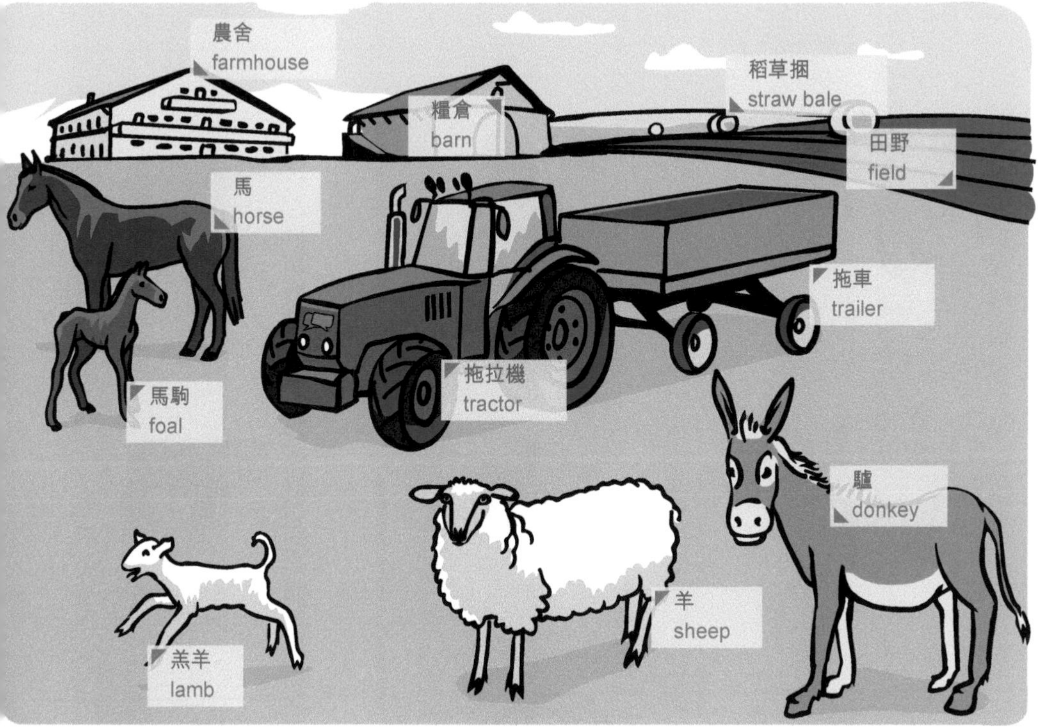
農舍
farmhouse
稻草捆
straw bale
糧倉
barn
田野
field
馬
horse
拖車
trailer
拖拉機
tractor
馬駒
foal
驢
donkey
羊
sheep
羔羊
lamb

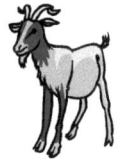

山羊

goat

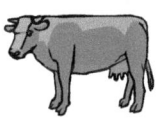

奶牛

cow

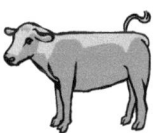

小牛

calf

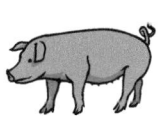

豬

pig

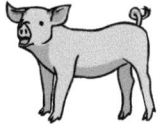

小豬

piglet

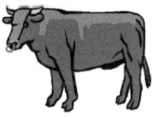

公牛

bull

鵝
goose

鴨
duck

小雞
chick

母雞
hen

公雞
cock

鼠
rat

貓
cat

老鼠
mouse

牛
ox

狗
dog

狗屋
doghouse

花園澆水軟管
garden hose

澆水壺
watering can

長柄大鐮刀
scythe

犁
plough

鐮刀
sickle

鋤頭
hoe

長柄草耙
pitchfork

斧頭
axe

獨輪手推車
wheelbarrow

飼料槽
trough

牛奶罐
milk can

麻布袋
sack

柵欄
fence

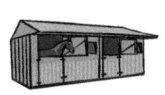

馬廄
stable

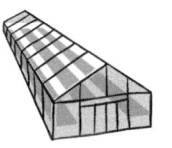

溫室
greenhouse

土壤
soil

種子
seed

肥料
fertilizer

聯合收割機
combine harvester

收割

harvest

收割

harvest

地瓜

yams

小麥

wheat

大豆

soy

土豆

potato

玉米

corn

油菜籽

rapeseed

果樹

fruit tree

樹薯

cassava

穀物

cereals

房子
house

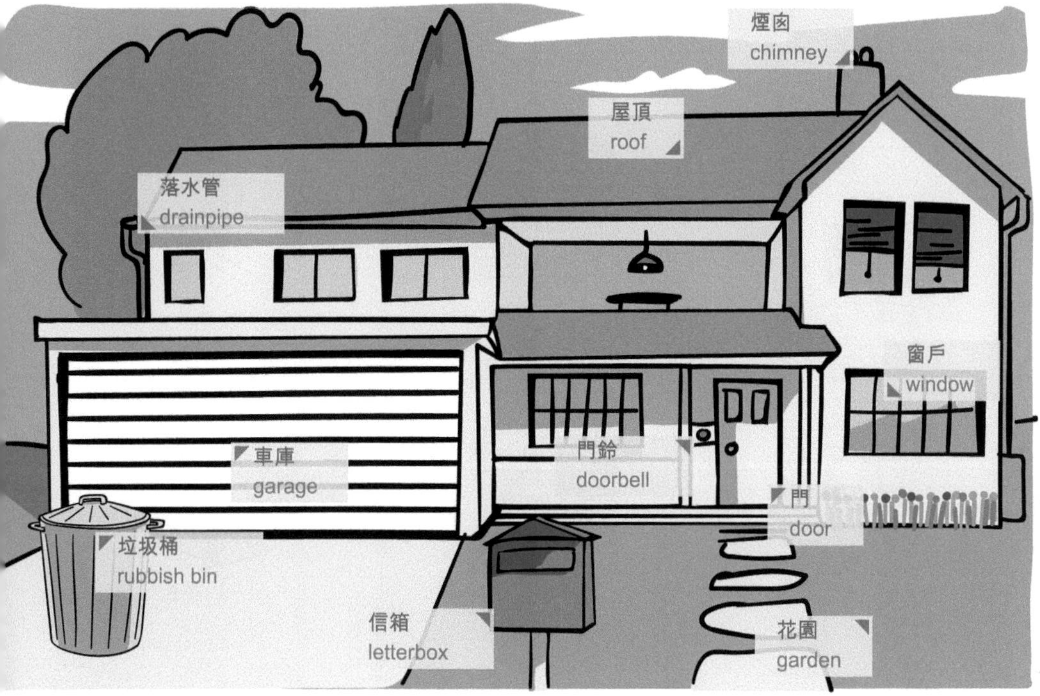

煙囪
chimney
屋頂
roof
落水管
drainpipe
窗戶
window
車庫
garage
門鈴
doorbell
門
door
垃圾桶
rubbish bin
信箱
letterbox
花園
garden

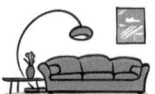

客廳
living room

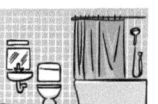

浴室
bathroom

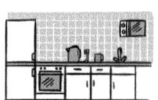

廚房
kitchen

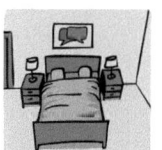

臥室
bedroom

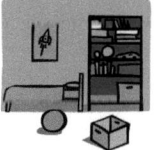

兒童房
child's room

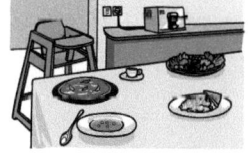

餐廳
dining room

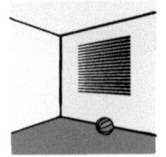

地板

floor

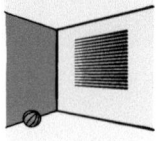

牆壁

wall

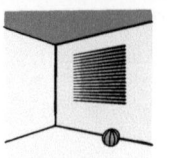

天花板

ceiling

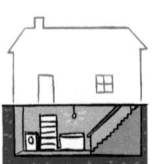

地窖

cellar

三溫暖

sauna

陽臺

balcony

露臺

terrace

游泳池

pool

割草機

lawn mower

被單

sheet

床罩

bedspread

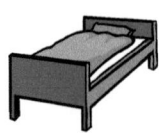

床

bed

掃帚

broom

水桶

bucket

開關

switch

客廳

living room

壁紙
wallpaper
相片
picture
檯燈
lamp
擱架
shelf
櫥櫃
cupboard
電視
television
壁爐
fireplace
花
flower
墊子
cushion
沙發
sofa
花瓶
vase
遙控器
remote control

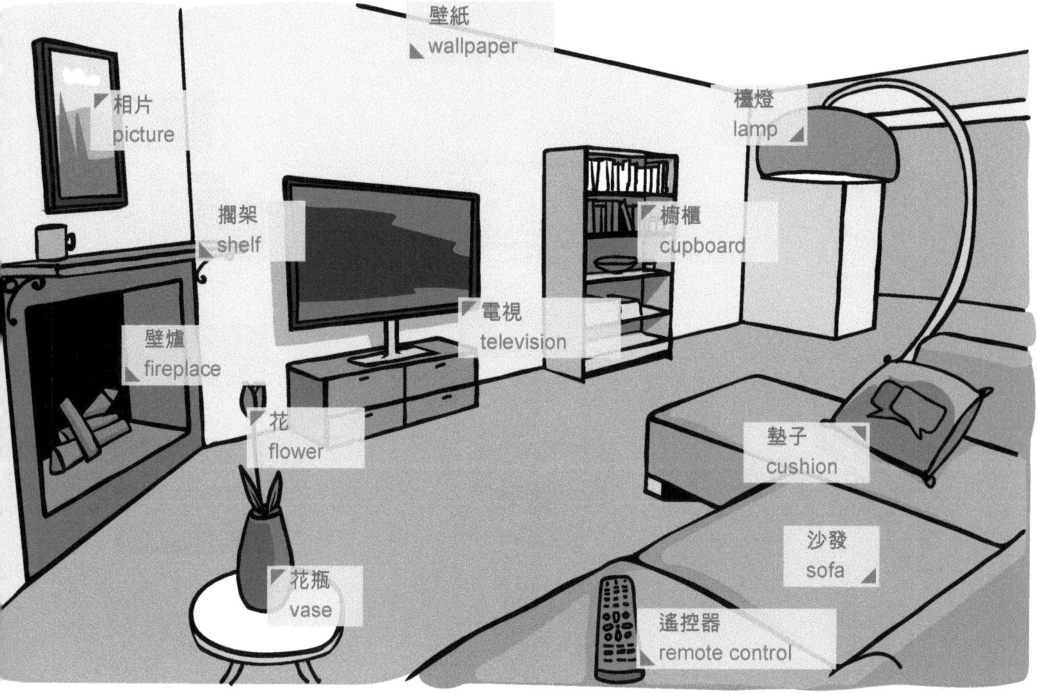

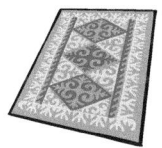

地毯

carpet

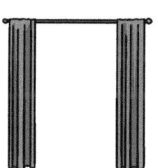

窗簾

curtain

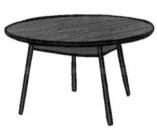

餐桌

table

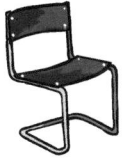

椅子

chair

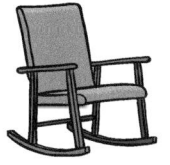

搖椅

rocking chair

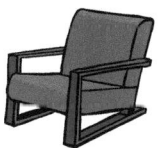

扶手椅

armchair

書
book

毯子
blanket

裝飾品
decoration

木柴
firewood

電影
film

高傳真音響
hi-fi equipment

鑰匙
key

報紙
newspaper

油畫
painting

海報
poster

收音機
radio

筆記本
notepad

吸塵器
hoover

仙人掌
cactus

蠟燭
candle

廚房
kitchen

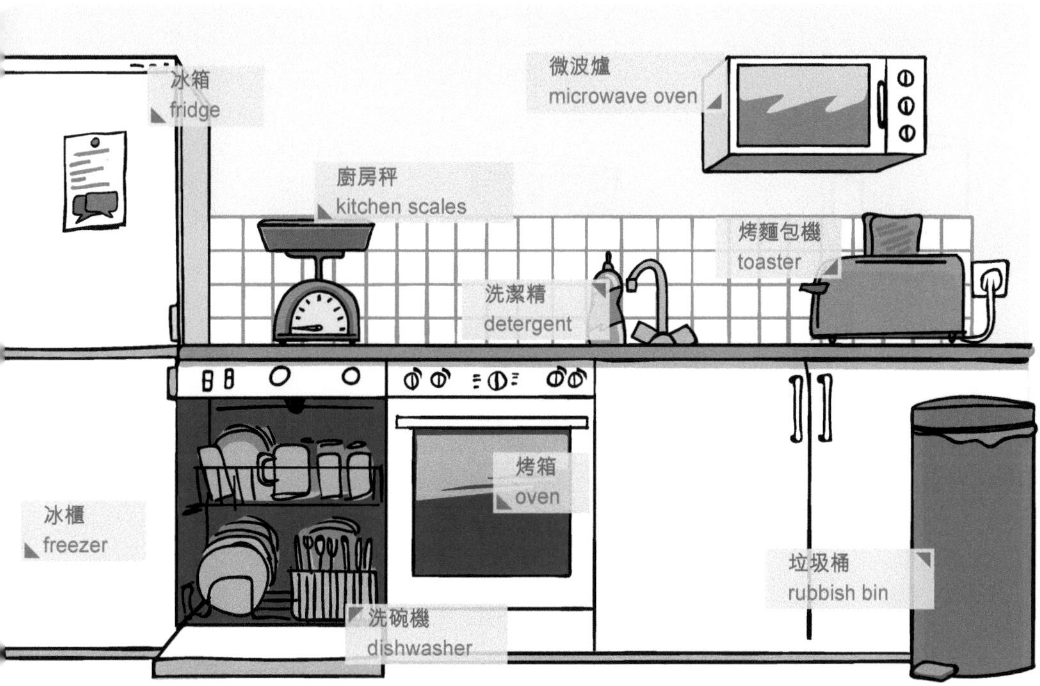
冰箱
fridge
微波爐
microwave oven
廚房秤
kitchen scales
烤麵包機
toaster
洗潔精
detergent
烤箱
oven
冰櫃
freezer
垃圾桶
rubbish bin
洗碗機
dishwasher

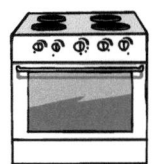

炊具

cooker

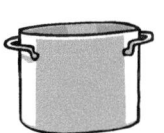

鍋

pot

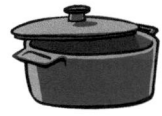

鑄鐵鍋

cast-iron pot

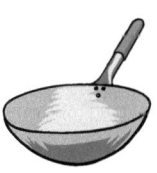

炒鍋

wok / kadai

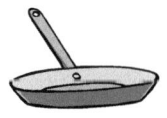

平底鍋

pan

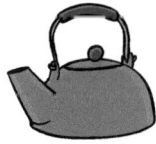

水壺

kettle

蒸鍋

steamer

烤盤

baking tray

陶瓷鍋

crockery

馬克杯

mug

碗

bowl

筷子

chopsticks

長柄勺

ladle

鏟子

spatula

攪拌器

whisk

濾網

strainer

篩子

sieve

磨碎機

grater

研缽

mortar

燒烤

barbecue

明火

open fire

菜板

chopping board

擀麵杖

rolling pin

開瓶器

corkscrew

罐子

can

開罐器

can opener

隔熱手套

pot holder

水槽

sink

刷子

brush

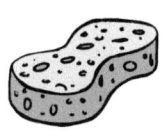

海綿

sponge

攪拌機

blender

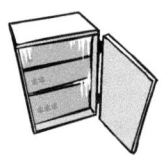

冷藏箱

deep freezer

奶瓶

baby bottle

水龍頭

tap

浴室
bathroom

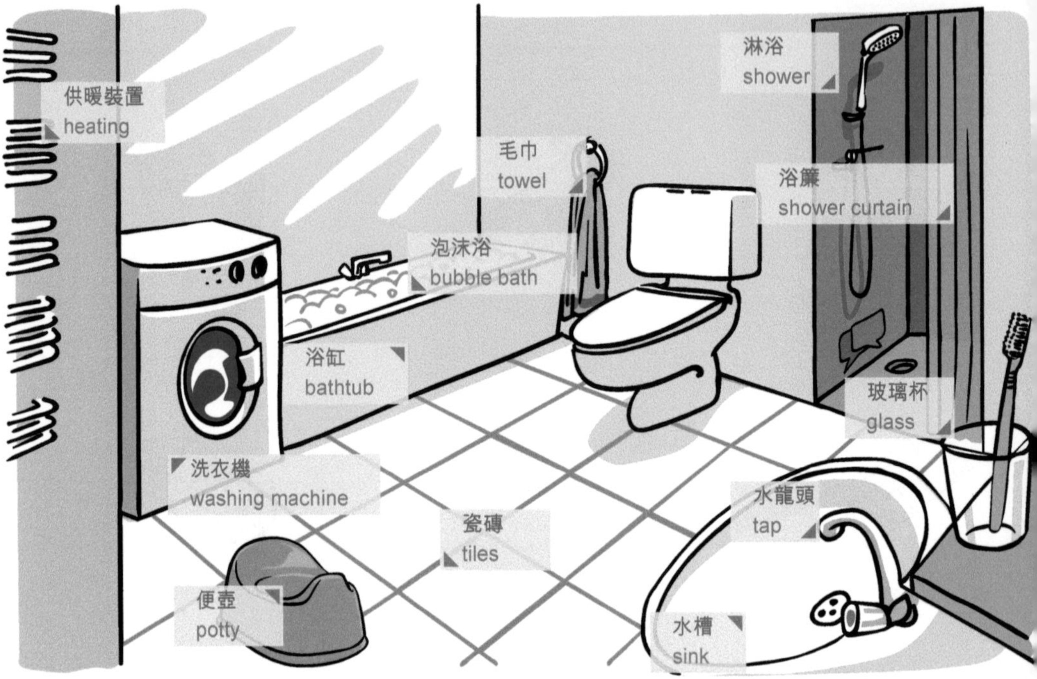

供暖裝置
heating

淋浴
shower

毛巾
towel

浴簾
shower curtain

泡沫浴
bubble bath

浴缸
bathtub

玻璃杯
glass

洗衣機
washing machine

瓷磚
tiles

水龍頭
tap

便壺
potty

水槽
sink

廁所
toilet

蹲便器
squat toilet

坐浴器
bidet

小便斗
urinal

廁紙
toilet paper

馬桶刷
toilet brush

牙刷

toothbrush

牙膏

toothpaste

牙線

dental floss

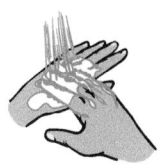

洗

wash

手持式蓮蓬頭

handheld shower

沖洗器

douche

洗臉盆

basin

洗背刷

back brush

肥皂

soap

沐浴露

shower gel

洗髮乳

shampoo

法蘭絨

flannel

排水

drain

乳霜

cream

除臭劑

deodorant

鏡子

mirror

手鏡

hand mirror

刮鬍刀

razor

刮鬍泡沫

shaving foam

鬍後水

aftershave

梳子

comb

刷子

brush

吹風機

hair dryer

噴髮定型劑

hairspray

化妝品

makeup

唇膏

lipstick

指甲油

nail varnish

化妝棉

cotton wool

指甲剪

nail scissors

香水

perfume

洗漱包
washbag

凳子
stool

計重秤
weighing scale

浴袍
bathrobe

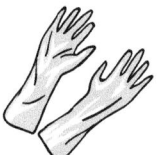

橡膠手套
rubber gloves

衛生棉條
tampon

衛生棉
sanitary towel

化學廁所
chemical toilet

兒童房
child's room

鬧鐘
alarm clock
毛絨玩具
cuddly toy
玩具車
toy car
撥浪鼓
rattle
玩具屋
doll's house
禮物
present

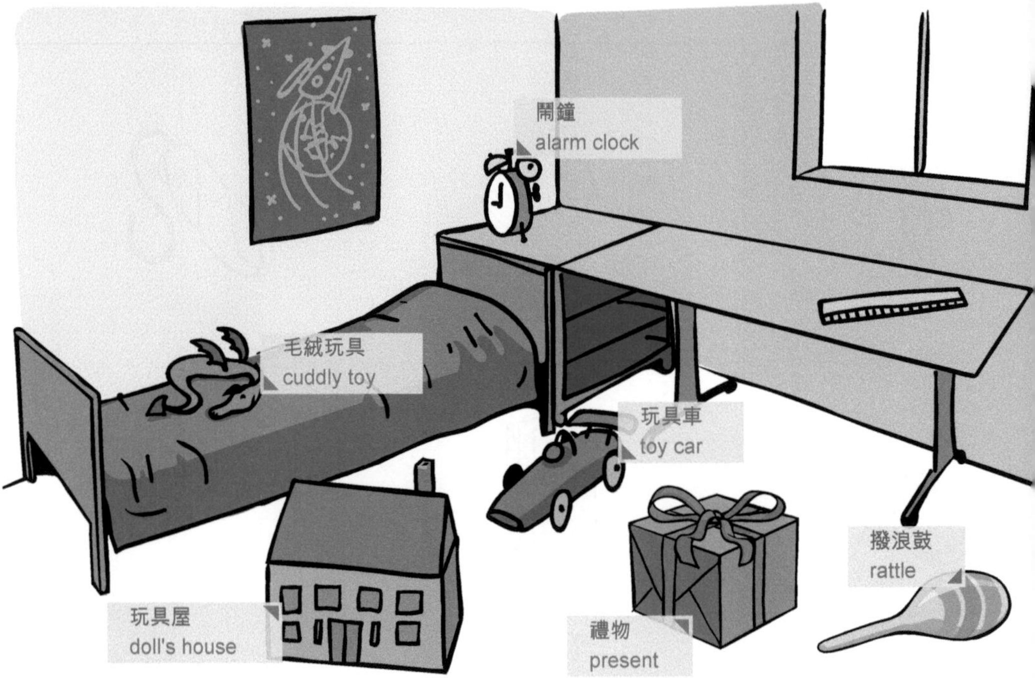

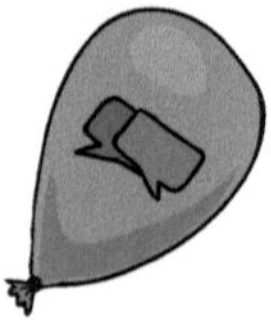

氣球

balloon

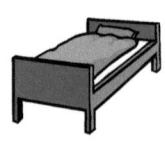

床

bed

嬰兒車

pram

撲克牌

deck of cards

拼圖

jigsaw

SUPER
MEGA

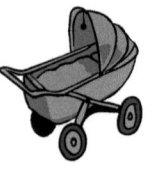

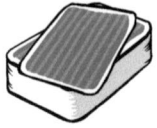

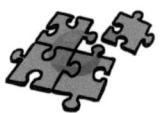

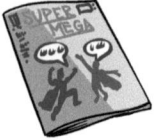

漫畫

comic

樂高積木

lego bricks

積木玩具

building blocks

公仔

action figure

嬰兒服

babygrow

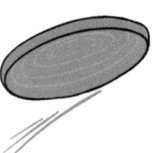

飛盤

frisbee

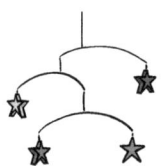

床鈴玩具

mobile

棋盤遊戲

board game

骰子

dice

火車模型

model train set

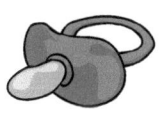

安撫奶嘴

dummy

派對

party

繪本

picture book

球

ball

洋娃娃

doll

玩

play

兒童房 - child's room　　43

沙坑

sandpit

鞦韆

swing

玩具

toys

電玩遊戲

video game console

三輪車

tricycle

泰迪熊

teddy bear

衣櫃

wardrobe

衣服
clothing

襪子

socks

長襪

stockings

緊身褲

tights

圍巾
scarf

雨傘
umbrella

皮帶
belt

T恤
t-shirt

靴子
boots

拖鞋
slippers

運動鞋
trainers

涼鞋
sandals

鞋
shoes

雨靴
rubber boots

內褲
underpants

胸罩
bra

背心
vest

身體

body

褲子

trousers

牛仔褲

jeans

短裙

skirt

女式襯衫

blouse

襯衫

shirt

套頭衫

pullover

連帽上衣

hoodie

西裝夾克

blazer

夾克

jacket

外套

coat

雨衣

raincoat

套裝

costume

連衣裙

dress

婚紗

wedding dress

西裝
suit

睡袍
nightgown

睡衣
pyjamas

莎麗
sari

頭巾
headscarf

包頭巾
turban

波卡
burqa

卡夫坦
kaftan

(阿拉伯式)長袍
abaya

泳衣
swimsuit

男式泳褲
trunks

短褲
shorts

運動服
tracksuit

圍裙
apron

手套
gloves

衣服 - clothing

鈕扣
button

眼鏡
glasses

手鏈
bracelet

項鍊
necklace

戒指
ring

耳環
earring

便帽
cap

衣架
coat hanger

帽子
hat

領帶
tie

拉鍊
zip

安全帽
helmet

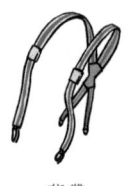

背帶
braces

校服
school uniform

制服
uniform

圍兜
bib

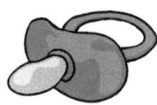

安撫奶嘴
dummy

尿布
nappy

辦公室
office

伺服器
server

檔案櫃
filing cabinet

印表機
printer

螢幕
monitor

紙
paper

滑鼠
mouse

辦公桌
desk

資料夾
folder

鍵盤
keyboard

廢紙簍
waste-paper basket

椅子
chair

電腦
computer

咖啡杯
coffee mug

計算機
calculator

網際網路
internet

筆記型電腦
laptop

信件
letter

簡訊
message

行動電話
mobile

網路
network

影印機
photocopier

軟體
software

電話
telephone

插座
plug socket

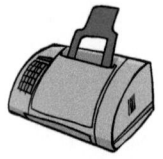

傳真機
fax machine

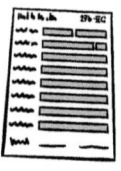

表格
form

檔案
document

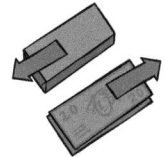

買

buy

付錢

pay

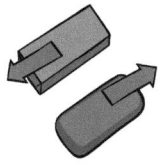

交易

trade

現金

money

美元

dollar

歐元

euro

日元

yen

盧布

rouble

瑞士法郎

Swiss franc

人民幣

renminbi yuan

盧比

rupee

提款處

cashpoint

外幣兌換處
bureau de change

金
gold

銀
silver

石油
oil

能源
energy

價格
price

合約
contract

稅金
tax

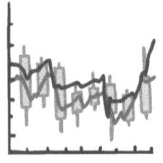

股票
stock

工作
work

職員
employee

老闆
employer

工廠
factory

商店
shop

經濟 - economy

警官
police officer

消防員
fireman

飛行員
pilot

醫師
doctor

廚師
cook

園丁
gardener

木匠
carpenter

裁縫
seamstress

法官
judge

化學家
chemist

演員
actor

公車司機

bus driver

計程車司機

taxi driver

漁夫

fisherman

清洗女工

cleaning lady

屋頂工

roofer

服務生

waiter

獵人

hunter

畫家

painter

麵包師

baker

電工

electrician

建築工人

builder

工程師

engineer

屠夫

butcher

水管工

plumber

郵差

postman

士兵

soldier

建築師

architect

收銀員

cashier

花農

florist

理髮師

hairdresser

售票員

conductor

機械技師

mechanic

船長

captain

牙醫

dentist

科學家

scientist

拉比

rabbi

伊瑪目

imam

和尚

monk

牧師

clergyman

工具

tools

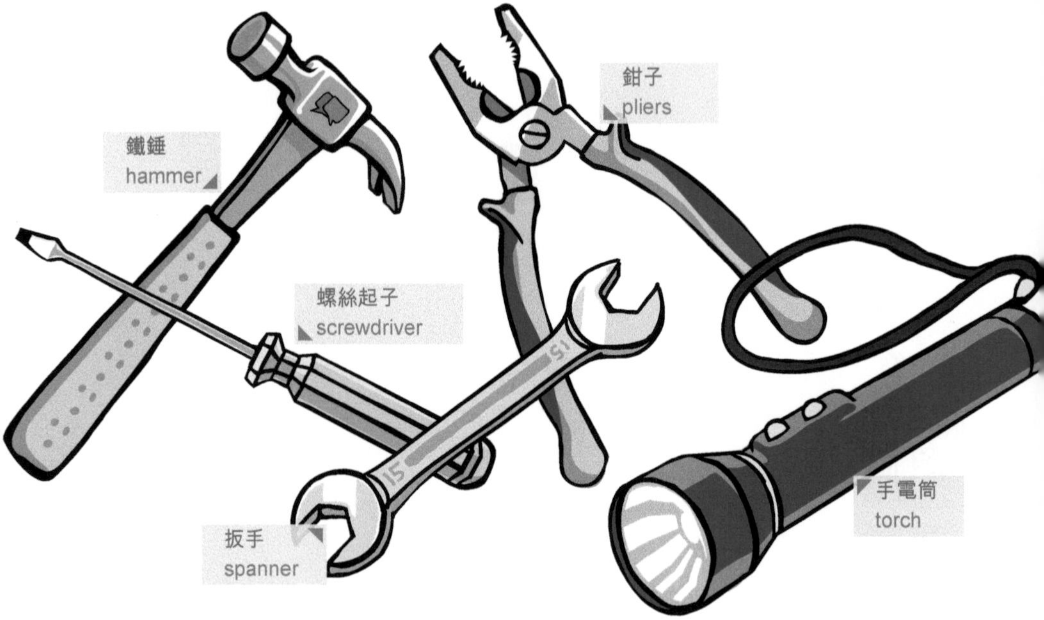
鐵錘
hammer
鉗子
pliers
螺絲起子
screwdriver
扳手
spanner
手電筒
torch

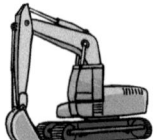

挖掘機

digger

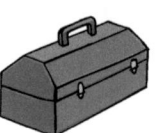

工具箱

toolbox

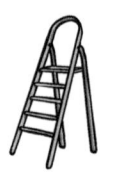

梯子

ladder

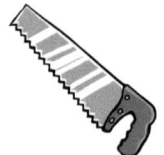

鋸子

saw

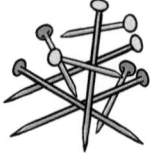

釘子

nails

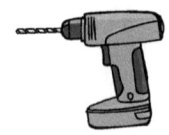

鑽機

drill

修
repair

鏟子
shovel

糟糕！
Damn!

畚箕
dustpan

油漆桶
paint pot

螺絲
screws

樂器

musical instruments

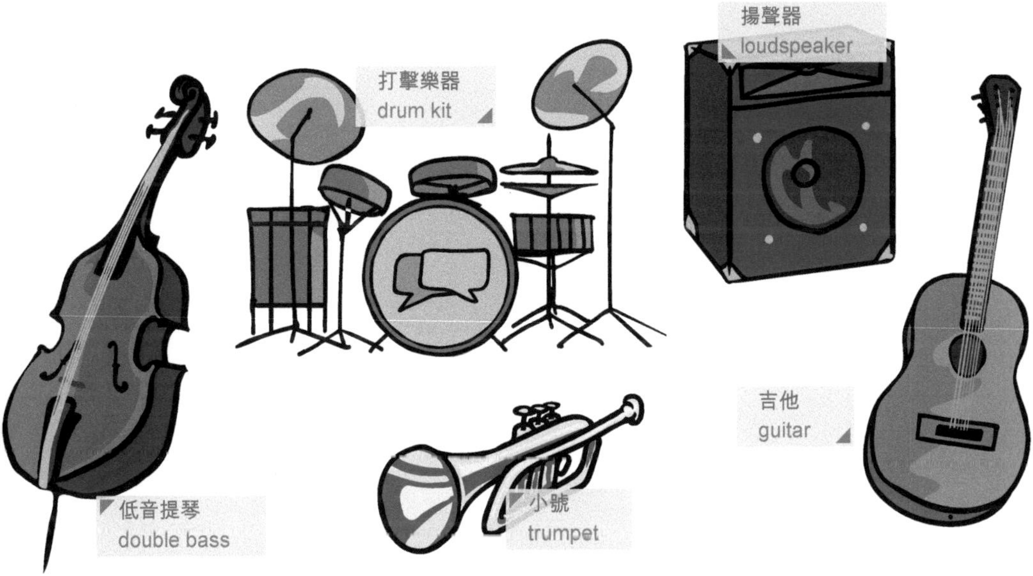

打擊樂器
drum kit

揚聲器
loudspeaker

吉他
guitar

低音提琴
double bass

小號
trumpet

鋼琴
piano

小提琴
violin

貝斯
bass

定音鼓
timpani

鼓
drums

電子琴
keyboard

薩克斯風
saxophone

長笛
flute

麥克風
microphone

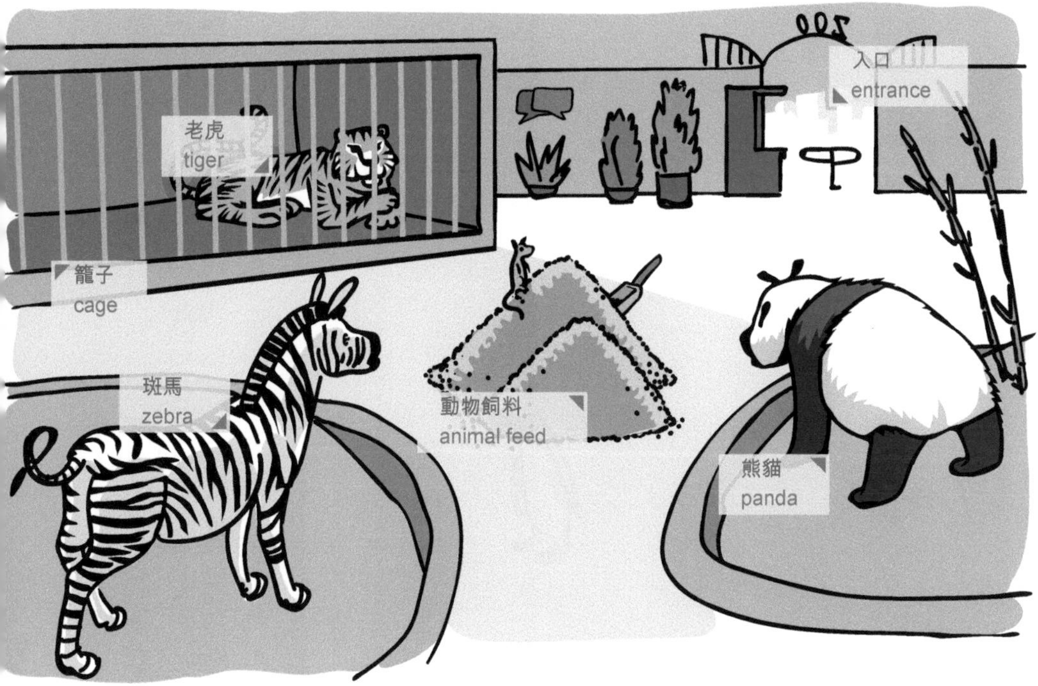
ZOO
入口
entrance
老虎
tiger
籠子
cage
斑馬
zebra
動物飼料
animal feed
熊貓
panda

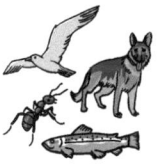

動物
animals

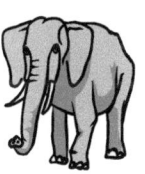

大象
elephant

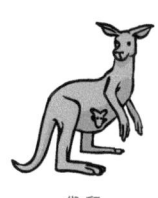

袋鼠
kangaroo

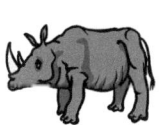

犀牛
rhino

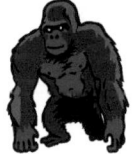

大猩猩
gorilla

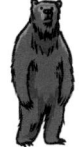

熊
bear

駱駝

camel

鴕鳥

ostrich

獅子

lion

猴子

monkey

紅鶴

flamingo

鸚鵡

parrot

北極熊

polar bear

企鵝

penguin

鯊魚

shark

孔雀

peacock

蛇

snake

鱷魚

crocodile

動物園管理員

zookeeper

海豹

seal

美洲豹

jaguar

矮種馬
pony

豹
leopard

河馬
hippo

長頸鹿
giraffe

老鷹
eagle

野豬
boar

魚
fish

龜
turtle

海象
walrus

狐狸
fox

羚羊
gazelle

橄欖球
American football

騎腳踏車
cycling

網球
tennis

籃球
basketball

游泳
swimming

拳擊
boxing

冰球
ice hockey

美式足球
football

羽毛球
badminton

田徑
athletics

手球
handball

滑雪
skiing

馬球
polo

跳 jump

擁抱 hug

笑 laugh

走路 walk

唱 sing

祈禱 pray

親吻 kiss

做夢 dream

書寫
write

畫
draw

展示
show

推
push

給
give

拿
take

有
have

做
do

當
be

站
stand

跑
run

拉
pull

丟
throw

摔倒
fall

躺
lie

等待
wait

攜帶
carry

坐
sit

穿衣
get dressed

睡覺
sleep

醒來
wake up

看
look at

哭
cry

擊
stroke

梳頭
comb

交談
talk

明白
understand

問
ask

聽
listen

喝
drink

吃
eat

清理
tidy up

愛
love

做飯
cook

開車
drive

飛
fly

航行
sail

計算
calculate

讀
read

學習
learn

工作
work

結婚
marry

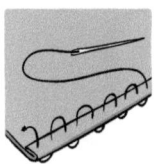

縫
sew

刷牙
brush teeth

殺
kill

抽菸
smoke

寄
send

祖母
grandmother

嬰兒
baby

母親
mother

祖父
grandfather

父親
father

女兒
daughter

兒子
son

客人
guest

阿姨
aunt

叔叔
uncle

兄弟
brother

姐妹
sister

身體

body

前額
forehead
眼睛
eye
肩膀
shoulder
手指
finger
臉
face
下巴
chin
手
hand
腿
leg
乳房
breast
手臂
arm

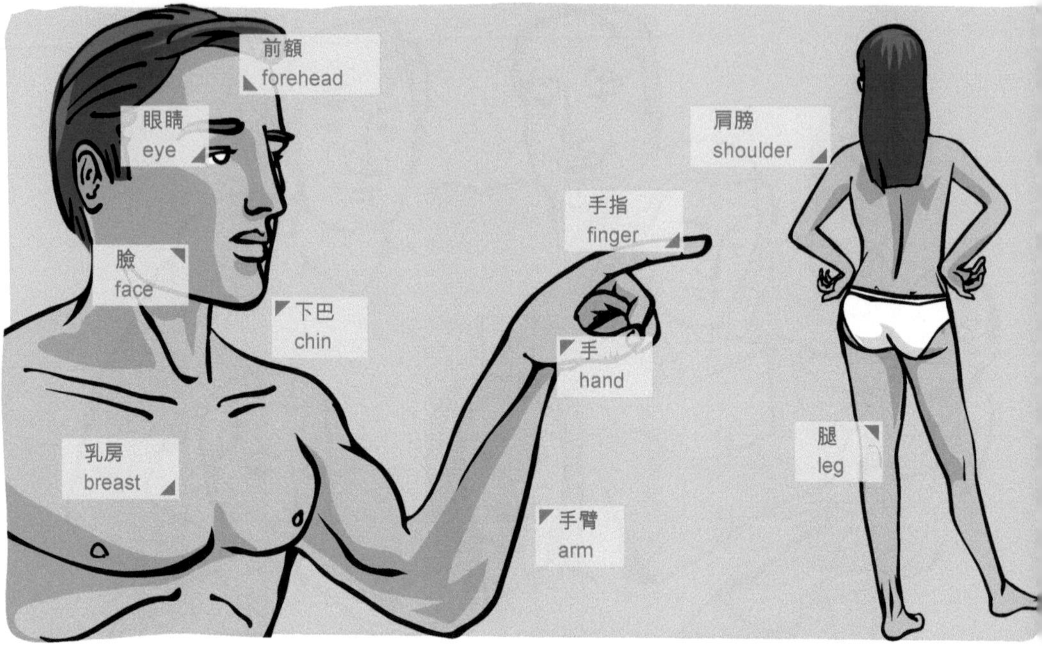

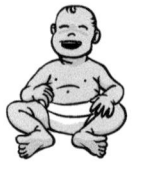

嬰兒
baby

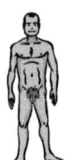

男人
man

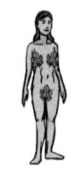

女人
woman

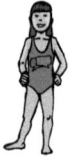

女孩
girl

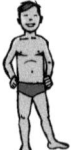

男孩
boy

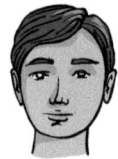

頭
head

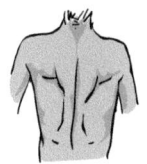

背部
back

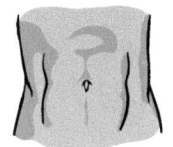

肚子
belly

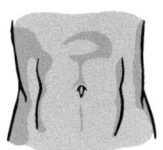

肚臍
belly button

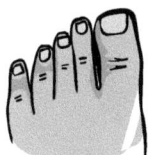

腳趾
toe

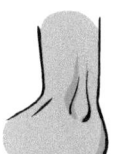

腳後跟
heel

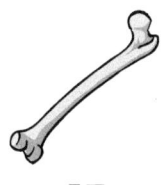

骨頭
bone

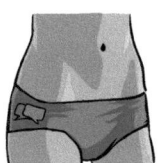

臀部
hip

膝蓋
knee

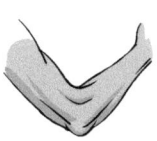

手肘
elbow

鼻子
nose

屁股
bottom

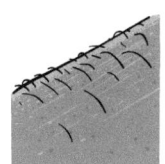

皮膚
skin

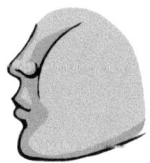

臉頰
cheek

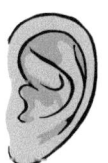

耳朵
ear

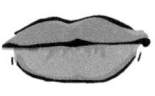

嘴唇
lip

身體 - body

嘴
mouth

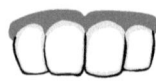

牙齒
tooth

舌頭
tongue

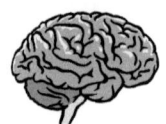

腦
brain

心臟
heart

肌肉
muscle

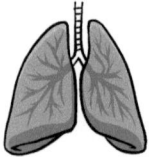

肺
lung

肝臟
liver

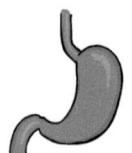

胃
stomach

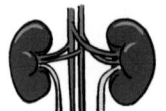

腎臟
kidneys

性交
sex

保險套
condom

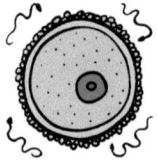

卵子
ovum

精子
semen

懷孕
pregnancy

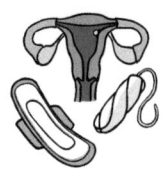

月事

menstruation

陰道

vagina

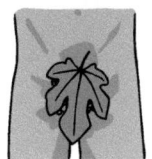

陰莖

penis

眉毛

eyebrow

頭髮

hair

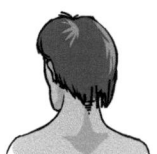

脖子

neck

醫院

hospital

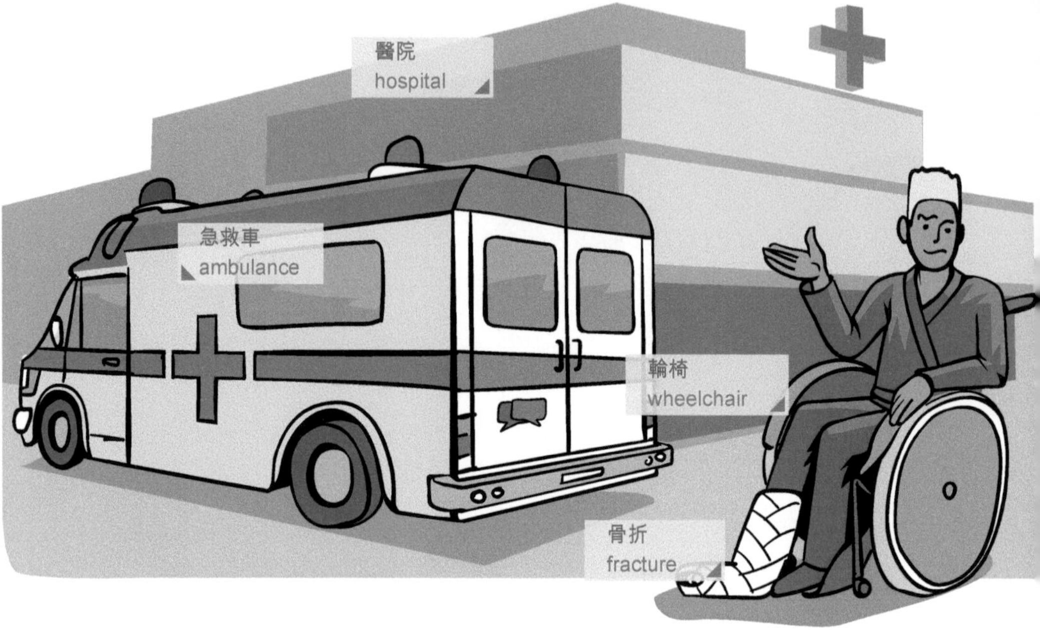

醫院
hospital
急救車
ambulance
輪椅
wheelchair
骨折
fracture

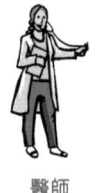

醫師
doctor

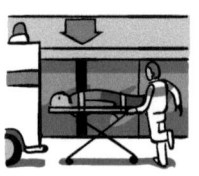

急診室
emergency room

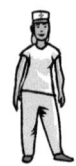

護理師
nurse

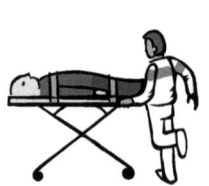

緊急情形
emergency

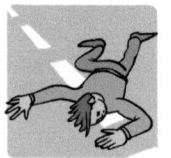

昏迷
unconscious

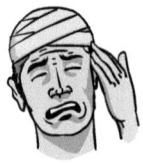

痛
pain

受傷
injury

出血
bleeding

心臟病發作
heart attack

中風
stroke

過敏
allergy

咳嗽
cough

發燒
fever

流感
flu

腹瀉
diarrhoea

頭痛
headache

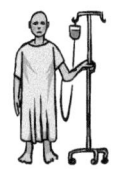

癌症
cancer

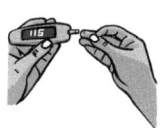

糖尿病
diabetes

外科醫師
surgeon

手術刀
scalpel

手術
operation

電腦斷層掃描
CT

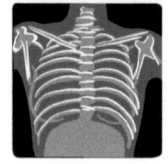

X光
x-ray

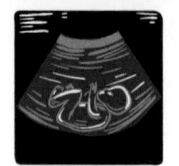

超音波
ultrasound

口罩
face mask

疾病
disease

候診室
waiting room

拐杖
crutch

石膏
plaster

繃帶
bandage

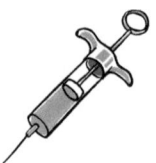

注射
injection

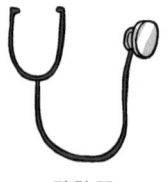

聽診器
stethoscope

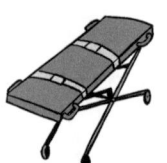

擔架
stretcher

體溫計
clinical thermometer

出生
birth

超重
overweight

醫院 - hospital

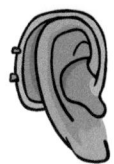

助聽器

hearing aid

消毒液

disinfectant

感染

infection

病毒

virus

愛滋病

HIV / AIDS

藥物

medicine

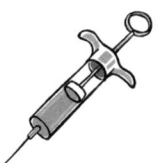

接種疫苗

vaccination

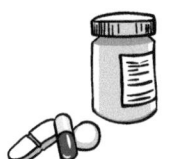

藥片

tablets

藥丸

pill

急救電話

emergency call

血壓計

blood pressure monitor

生病/健康

ill / healthy

救命！
Help!

警報
alarm

突擊
assault

攻擊
attack

危險
danger

緊急出口
emergency exit

失火了！
Fire!

滅火器
fire extinguisher

意外
accident

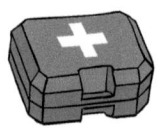
急救箱
first-aid kit

呼救訊號
SOS

員警
police

歐洲

Europe

北美洲

North America

南美洲

South America

非洲

Africa

亞洲

Asia

澳洲

Australia

大西洋

Atlantic

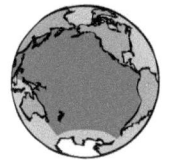

太平洋

Pacific

印度洋

Indian Ocean

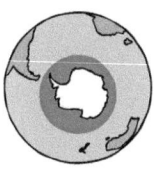

南冰洋

Antarctic Ocean

北冰洋

Arctic Ocean

北極

North Pole

南極

South Pole

南極洲

Antarctica

地球

Earth

陸地

land

海

sea

島

island

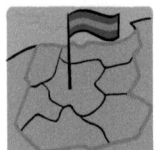

國家

nation

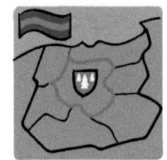

州

state

錶盤

clock face

時針

hour hand

分針

minute hand

秒針

second hand

現在幾點？

What time is it?

天

day

時間

time

現在

now

電子錶

digital watch

分

minute

時

hour

週

week

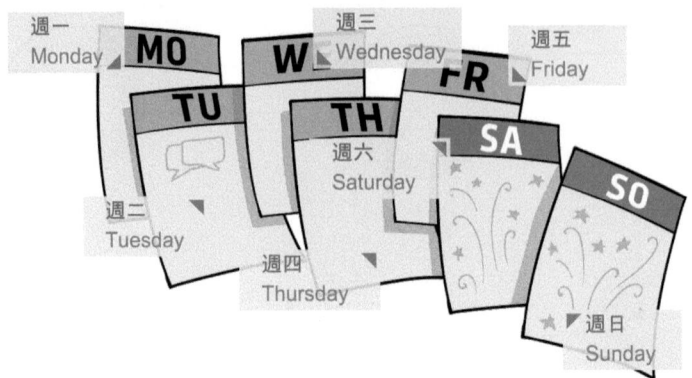

週一 Monday
週二 Tuesday
週三 Wednesday
週四 Thursday
週五 Friday
週六 Saturday
週日 Sunday

昨天

yesterday

今天

today

明天

tomorrow

早晨

morning

中午

noon

晚上

evening

工作日

business days

週末

weekend

年

year

雨
rain
彩虹
rainbow
風
wind
雪
snow
春
spring
秋
autumn
夏
summer
冬
winter

4.APRIL 11°
5.APRIL 4°
6.APRIL 13°
7.APRIL 8°
8.APRIL 10°

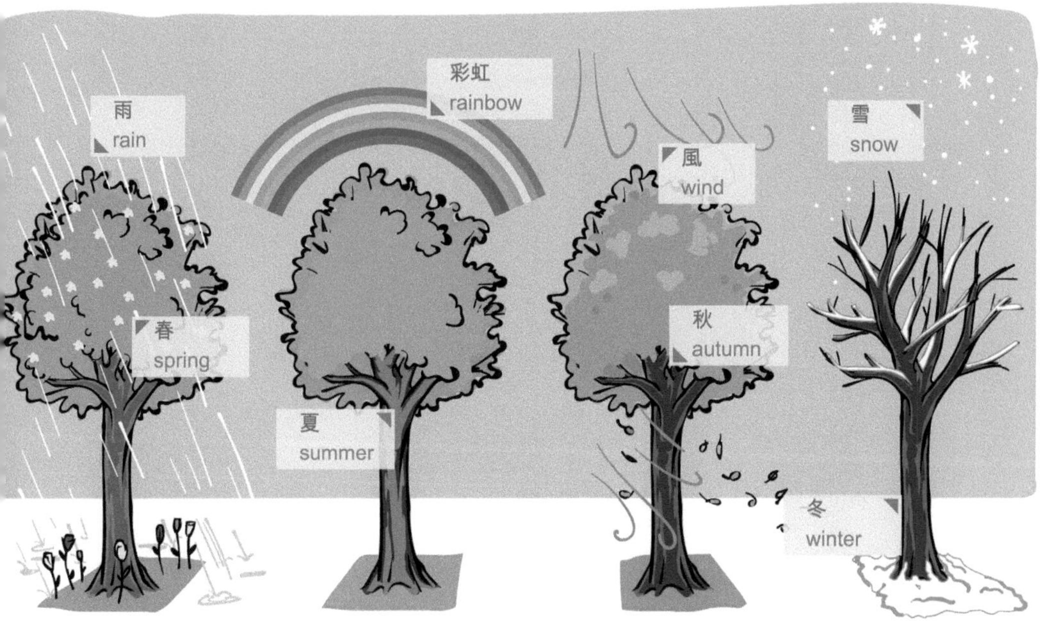

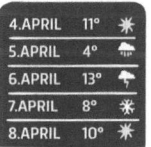

天氣預告

weather forecast

F
C
120
90
60
30
0
-30
40
30
20
10
0
-10
-20

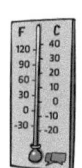

溫度計

thermometer

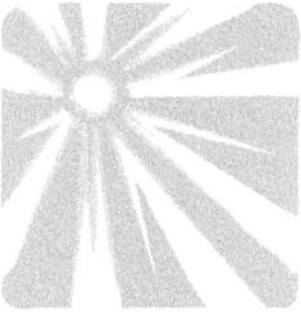

陽光

sunshine

雲

cloud

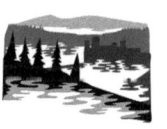

霧

fog

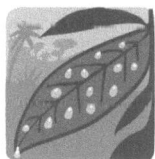

潮濕

humidity

閃電

lightning

打雷

thunder

風暴

storm

冰雹

hail

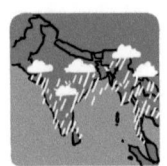

季風

monsoon

洪水

flood

冰

ice

一月

January

二月

February

三月

March

四月

April

五月

May

六月

June

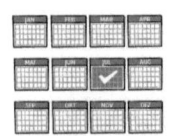

七月

July

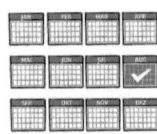

八月

August

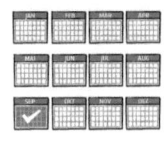

九月

September

十月

October

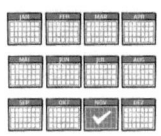

十一月

November

十二月

December

形狀
shapes

圓形

circle

正方形

square

長方形

rectangle

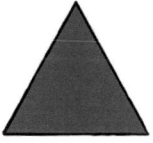

三角形

triangle

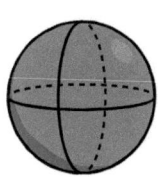

球體

sphere

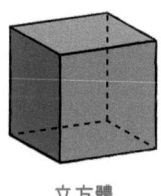

立方體

cube

白
....
white

黃
....
yellow

橙
....
orange

粉
....
pink

紅
....
red

紫
....
purple

藍
....
blue

綠
....
green

棕
....
brown

灰
....
grey

黑
....
black

很多/少許

a lot / a little

生氣/平靜

angry / calm

美/醜

beautiful / ugly

首/尾

beginning / end

大/小

big / small

明/暗

bright / dark

兄弟/姐妹

brother / sister

乾淨/骯髒

clean / dirty

完整/缺失

complete / incomplete

白天/晚上

day / night

死/生

dead / alive

寬/窄

wide / narrow

可食用/非食用

edible / inedible

邪惡/善良

evil / kind

興奮/無聊

excited / bored

胖/瘦

fat / thin

第一/最後

first / last

朋友/敵人

friend / enemy

滿/空

full / empty

硬/軟

hard / soft

重/輕

heavy / light

餓/渴

hunger / thirst

生病/健康

ill / healthy

非法/合法

illegal / legal

聰明/愚笨

intelligent / stupid

左/右

left / right

近/遠

near / far

新/舊

new / used

沒有/有些

nothing / something

老/幼

old / young

開/關

on / off

打開/闔上

open / closed

安靜/吵鬧

quiet / loud

富/窮

rich / poor

對/錯

right / wrong

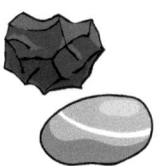

粗糙/光滑

rough / smooth

傷心/高興

sad / happy

短/長

short / long

慢/快

slow / fast

濕/乾

wet / dry

溫暖/涼爽

warm / cool

戰爭/和平

war / peace

反義詞 - opposites

0

零
....
zero

1

一
....
one

2

二
....
two

3

三
....
three

4

四
....
four

5

五
....
five

6

六
....
six

7

七
....
seven

8

八
....
eight

9

九
....
nine

10

十
....
ten

11

十一
....
eleven

12

十二
twelve

13

十三
thirteen

14

十四
fourteen

15

十五
fifteen

16

十六
sixteen

17

十七
seventeen

18

十八
eighteen

19

十九
nineteen

20

二十
twenty

100

百
hundred

1.000

千
thousand

1.000.000

百萬
million

英語

English

美式英語

American English

普通話

Chinese Mandarin

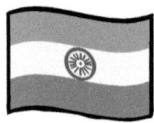

印地語

Hindi

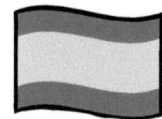

西班牙語

Spanish

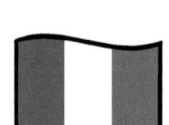

法語

French

阿拉伯語

Arabic

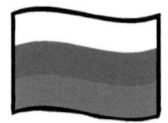

俄語

Russian

葡萄牙語

Portuguese

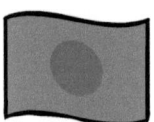

孟加拉語

Bengali

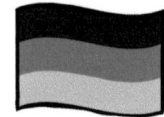

德語

German

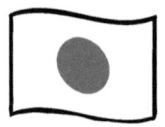

日語

Japanese

我
I

你
you

他/她/它
he / she / it

我們
we

你們
you

他們
they

誰？
who?

什麼？
what?

如何？
how?

何處？
where?

何時？
when?

名字
name

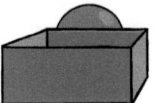

後面

behind

裡面

in

前面

in front of

上方

over

上面

on

下麵

under

旁邊

beside

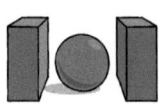

中間

between

地點

place